a Gospel Homecoming

40 Favorite Gospel Songs

Contents

Shawnee Press, Inc.

1107 17th Avenue South • Nashville, TN 37212

Visit Shawnee Press online at
www.shawneepress.com/songbooks

T0056049

FOREWORD

Homecoming…a chance to visit family and friends, share yummy foods, hilarious stories, fellowship and mostly, singing! Favorite songs make it just right for a cherished time that begs for another "homecoming" as everyone departs with hugs and promises of "let's do this again." I often tell young people to make good choices with those you spend the early years of your life, for those are the ones with whom you'll most likely spend your later years celebrating the memories of past days.

My favorite gospel songs surround homecoming memories. One funny such memory was the time my friend Tony Greene and his family, *The Greenes*, were asked to sing at a funeral. The grieving widow requested "Jingle Bells". After the group sang the holiday classic at the service, the widow said, "I am so sorry…I meant *When They Ring Those Golden Bells*."

Whether you're celebrating a "Heavenly Homecoming", a church homecoming or just playing and singing these songs for personal enjoyment, may the songs in this book bring a sense of peace, comfort, fellowship and "homecoming" to you!

—Judy Nelon
Compilation Consultant

Somebody Touched Me

Spiritual

Amazing Grace

John Newton; John P. Rees, stanza 5

Traditional American melody from
Carrell and Clayton's *Virginia Harmony*, 1831

Verse 3

The Lord has promised good to me,
His word my hope secures;
He will my shield and portion be
As long as life endures.

Verse 4

Thro' many dangers, toils, and snares
I have already come.
'Tis grace hath brought me safe thus far,
And grace will lead me home.

Verse 5

When we've been there ten thousand years,
Bright shining as the sun,
We've no less days to sing God's praise
Than when we'd first begun.

O Happy Day!

Philip Doddridge

Edward F. Rimbault

Verse 3

'Tis done, the great transaction's done,
I am my Lord's and He is mine;
He drew me, and I followed on,
Charmed to confess the voice divine.

Verse 4

Now rest, my long-divided heart,
Fixed on this blissful center, rest,
Nor ever from my Lord depart,
With Him of every good possessed.

Down by the Riverside

Traditional

Green Pastures
(Going to Live in Green Pastures)

Words and Music by
H. W. VanHoose

Every Time I Feel the Spirit

Spiritual

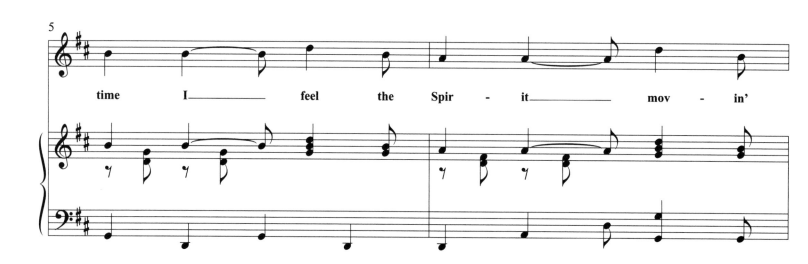

Hallelujah!

Words and Music by
Malcolm Jones

Jesus Is the Sweetest Name I Know

Words and Music by
Lela Long

Paradise Island

Words and Music by
Oakley Sharpe

The Sea Walker

Words and Music by
Tim Spencer

O, How I Love Jesus

Frederick Whitfield

Traditonal American melody

Verse 3

It tells me what my Father hath
In store for every day,
And, thoough I tread a darksome path,
Yields sunshine all the way.

Verse 4

It tells of One whose loving heart
Can feel my deepest woe,
Who in each sorrow bears a part
That none can bear below.

When Morning Sweeps the Eastern Sky

Words and Music by
O. A. Parris

I Bowed on My Knees and Cried "Holy"

Traditional

When They Ring the Golden Bells

Words and Music by
Daniel de Marbelle

Verse 3

When our days shall know their number,
And in death we sweetly slumber,
When the King commands the spirit to be free;

Nevermore with anguish laden,
We shall reach that lovely Eden,
When they ring the golden bells for you and me *(you and me).*

Oh, Come, Angel Band

Jefferson Hascall

William B. Bradbury

Church in the Wildwood

Words and Music by
William S. Pitts

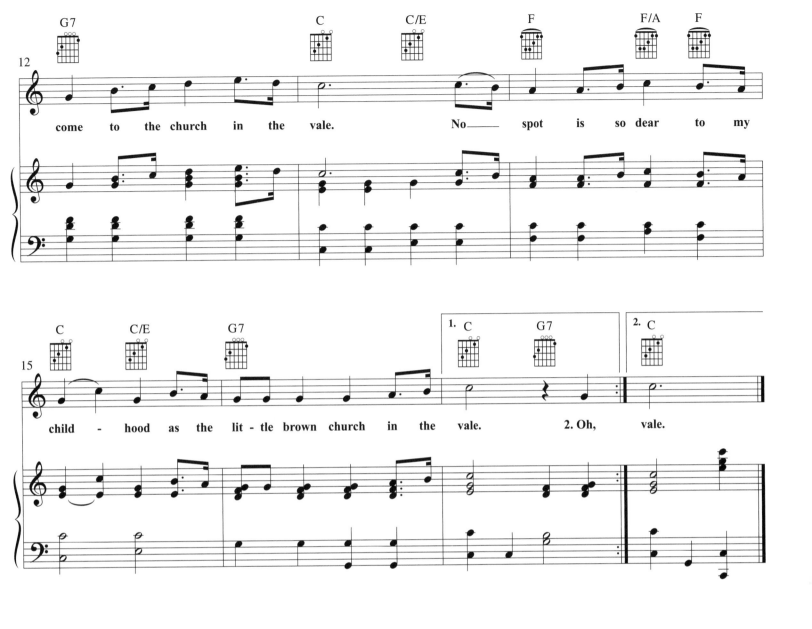

come to the church in the vale. No____ spot is so dear to my

child - hood as the lit - tle brown church in the vale. 2. Oh, vale.

Verse 3

From the church in the valley by the wildwood,
When day fades away into night,
I would fain from this spot of my childhood;
Wing my way to the mansions of light.

Deliverance Will Come

Traditional

Whispering Hope

Words and Music by
Alice Hawthorne

His Grace Reaches Me

Words and Music by
Whitey Gleason

With strength and warmth ♩ = 88

1. Deep - er_____ than the o - cean_____ and
2. High - er_____ than the moun - tains_____ and

wid - er_____ than the sea, is the grace of the
bright - er_____ than the sun, it was of - fered at

Sav - ior_____ for sin - ners_____ like me;
Cal - v'ry_____ for ev - 'ry - one;

Ivory Palaces

Words and Music by
Henry Barraclough

When the Roll Is Called Up Yonder

Words and Music by
James M. Black

1. When the trum-pet of the Lord shall sound and time shall be no more, And the
(2. On that) bright and cloud-less morn-ing when the dead in Christ shall rise, And the
(3. Let us) la-bor for the Mas-ter from the dawn till set-ting sun; Let us

morn-ing breaks, e-ter-nal, bright and fair; When the
glo-ry of His res-ur-rec-tion share; When His
talk of all His won-drous love and care. Then when

saved of earth shall gath-er o-ver on the oth-er shore, And the
cho-sen ones shall gath-er to their home be-yond the skies, And the
all of life is o-ver and our work on earth is done, And the

Blessed Assurance

Fanny J. Crosby

Phoebe P. Knapp

Verse 3

Perfect submission, all is at rest,
I in my Savior am happy and blest;
Watching and waiting, looking above,
Filled with His goodness, lost in His love.

Go, Tell It on the Mountain

Traditional Spiritual

Verse 3
Down in a lowly manger
the humble Christ was born
And brought us God's salvation
that blessed Christmas morn.

His Eye Is on the Sparrow

Civilla D. Martin

Charles H. Gabriel

He Keeps Me Singing

Words and Music by
Luther B. Bridgers

Verse 3
Feasting on the riches of His grace,
Resting 'neath His shelt'ring wing,
Always looking on His smiling face—
That is why I shout and sing.

Verse 4
Tho sometimes He leads thru waters deep,
Trials fall across the way,
Tho sometimes the path seems rough and steep,
See His footprints all the way.

Verse 5
Soon He's coming back to welcome me
Far beyond the starry sky;
I shall wing my flight to worlds unknown,
I shall reign with Him on high.

In the Garden

Words and Music by
C. Austin Miles

Verse 3
I'd stay in the garden with Him
Though the night around me be falling,
But He bids me go; through the voice of woe
His voice to me is calling.

Just Over in the Gloryland

James W. Acuff

Emmett S. Dean

o - ver in the glo - ry - land, There

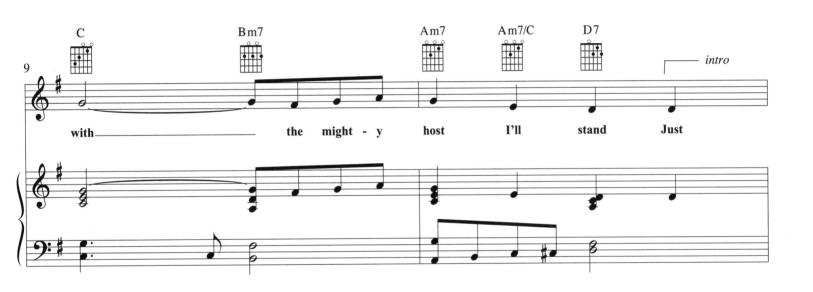

with_____ the might - y host I'll stand Just

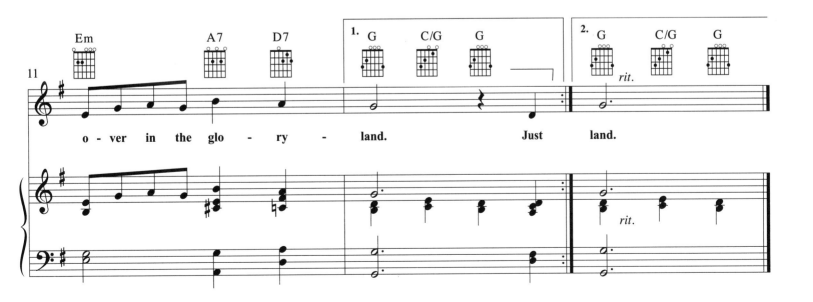

o - ver in the glo - ry - land. Just land.

Nearer, My God, to Thee

Sarah F. Adams

Lowell Mason

Verse 3

Or if, on joyful wing
Cleaving the sky,
Sun, moon, and stars forgot,
Upward I fly,

Still all my song shall be:
Nearer, my God, to Thee,
Nearer, my God, to Thee,
Nearer to Thee.

Leaning on the Everlasting Arms

Elisha A. Hoffman

Anthony J. Showalter

Verse 3
What have I to dread, what have I to fear,
Leaning on the everlasting arms?
I have blessed peace with my Lord so near,
Leaning on the everlasting arms.

O the Deep, Deep Love of Jesus

Samuel Trevor Francis

Traditional Gaelic melody

I Have Decided to Follow Jesus

Source unknown

Folk melody from India

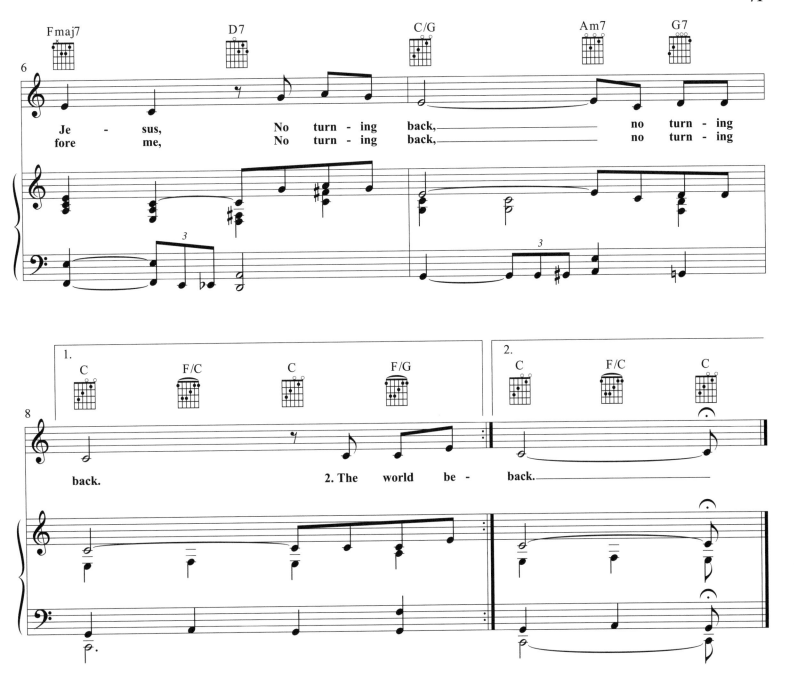

Verse 3

    Tho' none go with me, I still will follow,
    Tho' none go with me, I still will follow,
    Tho' none go with me, I still will follow,
    No turning back, no turning back.

Verse 4

    Will you decide now to follow Jesus,
    Will you decide now to follow Jesus,
    Will you decide now to follow Jesus?
    No turning back, no turning back.

Sweet Hour of Prayer

William W. Walford

William B. Bradbury

Lord, I'm Coming Home

Words and Music by
William J. Kirkpatrick

Verse 3

> I've tired of sin and straying, Lord—
> Now I'm coming home;
> I'll trust Thy love, believe Thy word—
> Lord, I'm coming home.

Verse 4

> My soul is sick, my heart is sore—
> Now I'm coming home.
> My strength renew, my hope restore—
> Lord, I'm coming home.

Rock of Ages

Augustus M. Toplady

Thomas Hastings

Verse 3

> Nothing in my hand I bring,
> Simply to Thy cross I cling;
> Naked, come to Thee for dress,
> Helpless, look to Thee for grace;
> Foul, I to the fountain fly,
> Wash me, Savior, or I die!

Verse 4

> While I draw this fleeting breath,
> When my eyes shall close in death,
> When I soar to worlds unknown,
> See Thee on Thy judgment throne,
> Rock of Ages, cleft for me,
> Let me hide myself in Thee.

Peace Like a River

Traditional

Energetic two ♩ = 90

1. I've got peace like a riv - er, I've got
(2. I've got) love like an o - cean, I've got

peace like a riv - er, I've got peace like a
love like an o - cean, I've got got peace love like an

riv - er in my soul;_____ I've got
o - cean in my soul;_____ I've got got

Verse 3

I've got joy like a fountain,
I've got joy like a fountain,
I've got joy like a fountain in my soul;

I've got joy like a fountain,
I've got joy like a fountain,
I've got joy like a fountain in my soul.

What a Friend We Have in Jesus

Joseph Scriven

Charles C. Converse

Verse 3

Are we weak and heavy-laden,
Cumbered with a load of care?
Precious Savior, still our Refuge,
Take it to the Lord in prayer.

Do thy friends despise, forsake thee?
Take it to the Lord in prayer;
In His arms He'll take and shield thee,
Thou wilt find a solace there.

There Is Power in the Blood

Words and Music by
Lewis E. Jones

Verse 3
Would you be whiter, much whiter than snow?
There's pow'r in the blood, pow'r in the blood;
Sin-stains are lost in its life-giving flow;
There's wonderful pow'r in the blood.

Verse 4
Would you do service for Jesus, your King?
There's pow'r in the blood, pow'r in the blood;
Would you live daily His praises to sing?
There's wonderful pow'r in the blood.

On Jordan's Stormy Banks

Samuel Stennett

Traditional American melody

Verse 3
No chilling winds nor poisonous breath
Can reach that healthful shore;
Sickness and sorrow, pain and death
Are felt and feared no more.

Verse 4
When shall I reach that happy place
And be forever blest?
When shall I see my Father's face
And in His bosom rest?

There Is a Fountain

William Cowper

Traditional American melody

1. There is a foun-tain filled with blood Drawn from Im-man-uel's veins, And sin-ners plunged be-neath that flood Lose all their guilt-y stains: Lose

(2. The) dy - ing thief re - joiced to see That foun - tain in his day, And there may I, though vile as he, Wash all my sins a - way: Wash

Verse 3

Dear dying Lamb, Thy precious blood
Shall never lose it pow'r,
Till all the ransomed Church of God
Be saved to sin no more;

Be saved to sin no more,
Be saved to sin no more;
Till all the ransomed church of God
Be saved to sin no more.

Verse 4

E'er since by faith I saw the stream
Thy flowing wounds supply,
Redeeming love has been my theme
And shall be till I die:

And shall be till I die,
And shall be till I die;
Redeeming love has been my theme
And shall be till I die.

Verse 5

When this poor lisping, stamm'ring tongue
Lies silent in the grave,
Then in a nobler, sweeter song
I'll sing Thy pow'r to save:

I'll sing Thy pow'r to save,
I'll sing Thy pow'r to save;
Then in a nobler, sweeter song
I'll sing Thy pow'r to save.

Where He Leads Me I Will Follow

E. W. Blandy

John S. Norris

Verse 3

I'll go with Him through the judgment,
I'll go with Him through the judgment,
I'll go with Him through the judgment,
I'll go with Him, with Him all the way.

Verse 4

He will give me grace and glory,
He will give me grace and glory,
He will give me grace and glory,
And go with me, with me all the way.